People are Talking

"Heartfelt, touching, raw, honest, irreverent, and funny."
— Madeleine Wild, Radio Magic, *How to be a Voiceover Success*

"Your characters are sympathetic, intriguing and frustrating, in other words, pure family. You told their tales with insight and compassion, weaving them together with a wonderful fabric of colorful words and observations, and your pace of storytelling was both hypnotic and rhythmic. You captured my skittery mind, entertained me, intrigued me, affected me, and enchanted me. Thank you for the honor and privilege of the early read. I LOVED it!"
— PJ Tyler, Cardinal Star Systems

"Sevenau's stories not only allow the reader to imagine a character's surroundings, but glimpse their inner landscape as well, and she does so with humor and compassion. She is a natural storyteller, and you often get the sense she is really telling on herself, which is why her writing is so compelling."
— David Gray, *Synergy, Sharksquill*

"I gave myself a Catherine fix last week, a writing festival of your work. I loved it. Your writings lead your readers into wanting more. Especially enjoyed your piece on your mother. Lots of talent, and I thank you for sharing."
— Elaine (Conway) Selmier

"Brave and tender stories that bless us by showing the cracks in our hearts."
— Carole Peccorini, *Conversations That Matter*

"Your writing style is compelling. It's easy to read; I hear your voice, almost feel your "Catherine-ness." I smile at the way you poke fun at our human condition. Your sense of humor is delightful, particularly in your playful, gentle use of sarcasm to highlight the quirky affliction of being human. I feel more accepting of myself and my own shortcomings as a result of reading your work, and I love it for that reason alone."
— Chell Atchley

D0619846

To Evelyn, a friend and fellow queen!

Passages from
Behind These Doors
A Family Memoir

Catherine Sevenau

by Catherine Sevenau

Passages from Behind These Doors: A Family Memoir

© 2014 Catherine (Clemens) Sevenau
Sevenau.com
CSevenau@earthlink.net

ISBN-13: 978-0615971605

Publisher:
Tintype Publishing
P.O. Box 1206
Sonoma, CA 95476

Editor:
Deb Carlen
Five-Ideas.com

Design & Layout:
Todd Towner
TandHGraphics.com

Author Photos:
InHerImagePhoto.com

Voice Director:
Madeleine Wild (audio version)
RadioMagic.com

Sound Engineer:
Roy Blumenfeld
RadioMagic.com

Cover Design:
Dianna Jacobsen
DiannaJacobsen.com

Cover Illustration:
Mary Patterson
Fishchild.com

Acknowledgements

Writing a book is not a solitary event, and this one would not have emerged without my friend and teacher, Stephanie Moore. Years ago she taught me to dance, then she taught me to write. I thank my Monday night writing class who gave me their attention and feedback, a page and a half at a time. Thanks to my siblings and friends who generously read my drafts, edited my commentary, encouraged me, and nudged me to get to the point. I'm deeply indebted to my mentor, Michael Naumer, who taught me that where I am the most wounded, I am the most accomplished; that work gave me the perspective to write this book as more than just a story. Thanks to my editor, Deb Carlen, who put the final polish on these twenty tales, to Todd Towner, who formatted them for publishing, and to my voice over coach, Madeleine Wild, who helped me deliver them in my own voice.

Twenty Passages from

Behind These Doors
A Family Memoir

Table of Contents

Teller of Tales

This tale is a history, a fable, a prayer
of those gone before me, now gathered with care.
The diaries and pictures and letters enclosed
deciphered my kin and what they supposed.
Those who are living—their stories intact,
Those gone before us—who knows what was fact!
I met not the aunts nor uncles you'll greet,
met not the grandparents whose waltz is complete.
I presume who they were by looking at me—
our blossoms and thorns twining through this same tree.
Our shadows and secrets for so long passed down,
those thistles and thorns, now replaced by a crown.
It was back in the thirties my parents did meet,
then married, had children with ten little feet.
I am the youngest, this teller of tales,
unearthing my family, removing our veils.
I'm descended from Clemens, the kin of my dad
who married a Chatfield—a girl some thought bad.
I've written of both, their histories and lives,
of Mom's other husband and Daddy's three wives.
I know they'll excuse me—my gaffes and asides,
'tis those who are living who might have my hide.
I wrote of my brother, my sisters and me,
recording our stories with hazed memory.
Some snort and are angry, they threaten and rear—
There are nights I don't sleep from the scorn that I fear.
But it's none of my business what they think of me—
I wrote what I deemed 'bout this family tree.

by Catherine (Clemens) Sevenau

Behind These Doors
A Family Memoir

1. Prologue

My brother Larry was under the illusion that our mother was a good mother, but he had a different childhood than the rest of us. My sisters were convinced otherwise: Carleen complained Mom was thoughtless and self-centered, Betty resented her for abandoning us, and Claudia simply thought she was weak—all of which was true by the way. I was never under the illusion I had a bad mother, I was under the illusion I had the wrong mother, and although I was not under the illusion she loved me, I hoped she might someday. I was raised by omission, but neglect doesn't leave a scar, it leaves a hole. Some say holes are harder to heal. Fortunately, I only lived with her from the time I was five until the age of nine. I figure that's why I'm not completely neurotic. Or dead.

Clemens siblings, 1950, Sonora, California
L-R: Carleen, Claudia, Cathy (Catherine) in middle front, Betty (Liz), Larry (Gordon)

I wrote our story, which evolved into a five-year journey. A magnitude of personal growth work put it into perspective; a writing class helped me get it down on paper. It's about doors opened, closed, and locked, and about a family so complicated you'll need a scorecard. As my friend Billy says, "There are really only five-hundred people on the planet, the rest are just crowd scenes done with mirrors." It seems I'm friends with, or related to, most of these people. The rest I've dated.

My siblings loved my writing. Then a change of heart on my sister's part, regarding something she said I could use, caused a major rift. So as not to be cast out, and to honor her wishes, I put the book away. For the next five years I worked on our genealogy. It was safer; they were all dead. My sister has since passed, along with enough time, so I returned to finishing "the book."

What follows is what I've been told, what I recall, and what my family claims I've made up. Some stories I've never disclosed; some I've recounted so many times I can't remember if they're even true anymore. But do we ever recollect what actually happened? Certainly we remember our version—and what we believe is true for us, so we better be careful what we believe. And does any of it matter? Only when we make it mean something.

Clemens siblings: Claudia, Catherine, Liz, Gordon, Carleen, 1989

2. The Golden Eagle Café, 1932, Colusa, California

On a crisp fall morning after Mass, Carl and Lawrence Clemens perched on the swivel stools at the Golden Eagle Cafe. The brothers made small talk with the proprietor, Mrs. Nellie Chatfield, as she served their usual Sunday breakfast of fried bacon and eggs. And then, Babe walked in. Mrs. Chatfield's sixteen-year-old daughter seldom showed up any morning before 10:00. She liked to sleep in.

Babe, Nellie Chatfield, Fred Chamberlain (Nellie's brother),
1932 at the Golden Eagle Cafe

Lawrence and Carl came to Colusa in August, 1932, to work on the construction of the new weir. Employed by Frederickson & Watson Construction Company, traveling from job to job, they roomed in boarding houses wherever their work took them. They became Sunday morning regulars, and Babe always waited for them before making her entrance down the stairs. She sat at a nearby table while her mother cooked her a steak, rare. Lawrence sat at the end of the counter, eyeing her. Babe was sharp-tongued, fast-talking, quick to flirt, and even quicker to laugh. He thought she was one snappy girl.

Of the two lanky men, Lawrence was the talker, and he was the one who bantered back and forth with her, laughing and telling stories. Carl said little when Babe was nearby; he may have been twenty-six—

and seven years older than Lawrence—but he still had the innocence of a farm boy.

The brothers missed their family and home-cooked food. They liked coming to the café and they liked Mrs. Chatfield. She reminded them of their mother; she too believed in God, hard work, and common sense. They respected that in a woman. In return, Nellie Chatfield admired the men, especially Carl. He was Catholic, dependable, quiet and kind, and he didn't smoke or drink. This man was a good prospect for her daughter. He would be a decent addition to the family: yes, Carl Clemens was a grand choice in Nellie Chatfield's book. If only she was younger.

Nellie Chatfield

Comfortable around Mrs. Chatfield, Carl and she discussed the heat and the bugs, the differences between hay and rice farming, and went on and on about Longhorns and Leghorns. They could talk about almost anything. It was Babe he was tongue-tied around. His sweaty palms wouldn't come out of his pockets when she was near, his long legs stayed wrapped and glued to the swivel chair post, his large feet locking him on.

Even though Lawrence thought Babe was spoiled, getting up late and being waited on hand and foot by her mother, he was drawn to her. She was not like the Catholic girls back home, not like any girls he knew. She seemed older, bolder, and more outspoken. But Lawrence didn't interest Babe—Carl did. Carl, who didn't say a word to her, who could hardly look her in the eye, who bowed his head, lowered his lashes and twiddled his thumbs whenever she came near. But Babe wasn't used to being ignored. She set her sights on this good-looking Minnesota farmer, determined to have him, and went after Carl like Annie Oakley roping a

Lawrence Clemens   Carl Clemens

rodeo calf. He never even felt the branding. Too shy and naive to make a move on his own, he was roped and tied before he hit the ground.

Lawrence, upset about their impending marriage, did everything he could to talk his brother out of it.

"This woman is not going to be good for you," he warned. "She's not the kind of woman to marry. She'll only cause you heartache and trouble." Carl turned a deaf ear.

And so, within six months of meeting one another in the Golden Eagle Cafe, in an early morning Mass at Our Lady of Lourdes Catholic Church in Colusa, my father married my mother.

As it turned out, Lawrence wasn't jealous. He was right.

Noreen "Babe" Chatfield

3. Sin and Prayer

My parents were like black and white, oil and water, sin and prayer. Daddy, not one to boil over, married a bubbling kettle of emotions. If he could've loosened his grip and if my mother hadn't unraveled, my childhood might've been different.

I got the best of my father, inheriting his common sense, work ethic, and reliability, and managed to get the worst of my mother, sporting her self-absorption, stinginess, and pride. I possess his conduct and character, bear her entitlement and disdain. I have Daddy's loyalty, Mom's indifference, his modesty, her vanity, his respectfulness, her sarcasm. I carry his confidence and live with her self-doubt.

Until I'd met some Chatfield cousins at a reunion, I'd seldom come across anyone in the family who said anything good about Mom. I was confused at first, thinking they were mixing her up with one of her sisters as they referred to her as "Babe" rather than Noreen. My cousins remembered her when she was young. They admired Mom, and thought she was honest, humorous, and even hip. They told me she was smart and could hold her own on almost any subject, that she was well-read in history, loved plays and concerts, and was keen on sports, able to rattle off team stats with the best of them. It was really nice to know that she had people in her court.

Sharing their stories made me realize that my mother wasn't as "out there" as I'd thought; she was just like the rest of her family, who were all a little out there. I liked hearing about her younger years, when she was different from the mother I knew.

Babe was not the mother I wanted, but she was the one I got. Was she a good mother? Not by the time I came along. Did I love her? No, I can't say I did. I imagine Babe would've wanted things to turn out differently, to not have stumbled and tripped through life, leaving a batch of broken and chipped china in her path. But having her as a parent turned out to be in my best interest, and though it took me years to see it, my experiences growing up were actually happening *for* me, not *to* me. Although she may not have been "good enough," I turned out as well as I have because stand-ins appeared throughout my life: sisters and friends and lovers who filled that mothering gap for me.

I survived my childhood, grew up, and raised two sons as a single mom. I went from welfare to two successful businesses and a longtime career in real estate.

I learned to dance, no small feat for someone with two left ones, and I wrote this book. It gave me a vehicle to express my thoughts, and offered me a mirror to see myself.

Mother only wanted the same things I want: to be seen and to be heard. Writing this book did that, for both of us.

Sons: Matt and Jon Sevenau
1975, Sonoma

Jon, Catherine, Matt Sevenau
2007, Sonoma

4. If It's Not One Thing… It's Your Mother

We think our life is someone else's fault. As victims of circumstance, blown by fate and buffeted by winds, we need somebody to pin it on. Our father often takes the heat, but usually it's our mother. We also blame the schools, the government, and the past. If it has anything to do with missing homework, we blame the dog. If we're dyslexic, we blame God—unless of course you were raised in a happy-clappy church. I wasn't. I was raised Roman Catholic, the religion of rules and reservations, especially about sex.

Once we find someone to take the fall, we squander our life living in *if only*. We waste our energy wandering along the yellow brick road and wailing: the sky is falling, the sky is falling! Bonding with doom and gloom, grist and gossip, bad news, bad skin, and bad hair, we become skeptical and cynical, residing in complacency and complaint.

Cathy Clemens
1949, Sonora

This all started when we were small children and separated from the soul with which we were born, when our spirit was quashed. Oh to be able to reconnect with that sweet soul we left behind; if we could, perhaps the world, our small piece of it anyway, would make more sense. We could be ourselves again.

It only takes a slight course adjustment to reach a different destination, and I'm two-stepping on a repaved path. I can't change my history, genetic blueprint, or my family, but I can change how I choose to live my life. So I practice breathing, and living inside my body. I practice gratitude and generosity. I practice patience. The rest of the time I just try not to holler at everyone.

In the journeys of my life—from wondering how I got here to knowing where I am, from falling down the rabbit hole to dancing with the stars, from having my mother show up in my stomach, bones, and dreams to writing a book about her so as to meet her, and meeting myself instead—I find I'm not about the pearl, but about the sand that made me. Mine was not the childhood I wished for, but who am I to question grace?

5. Nothin' But Trouble • August 1948, Sonora, California

Plucked from my mother's womb, I missed the struggle from one world to another with no heroic journey or victorious birth cry. No wonder I don't know how I got here. I was short-circuited from the beginning.

Just after midnight, Mom gave birth to me by optional cesarean, which was in vogue if you were wealthy. We weren't. She wanted to have her tubes tied so Dad wouldn't know, and Mom's doctor was willing to do it for her. If she had it done while having a cesarean, no one would know. It was illegal for him to perform this kind of surgery without the husband's permission and it could've gotten them both in a lot of hot water. He'd been my mother's doctor for years and knew it would be the end of her if she had another child. Mom was not concerned about it being against the law or a mortal sin. She was barely hanging on to her soul as it was.

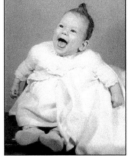

Cathy Clemens, 1948

I was welcomed into the family two years after Mom's first breakdown, but not by her. She didn't want another child; she wanted out. As far as she was concerned, I was a fifth burden, tacking on another eighteen years to her prison sentence. Another eighteen years of not wanting to be a wife or a mother, not wanting to cook and clean and cry every day.

None of the kids knew Mom was pregnant, and apparently it hadn't occurred to my parents that questions might arise upon my arrival. Larry was a fourteen-year-old boy and clueless. Carleen, who was thirteen, found out in catechism the month before I was due. Stunned, she said, "Not my mother!" She knew you had to have sex to have a baby and she could hardly imagine her parents doing such a thing. Betty, now nine, was off climbing fences and protecting the weak, but took the news in stride; I would be her next foundling.

Larry, Carleen, Betty, Claudia, 1948, Yosemite

Claudia, who was seven, found out when Larry told her she had a new sister. She was excited, but that was before discovering she wasn't allowed to play with me. Claudia was curious to see what I was all about, but was constantly reprimanded, "Don't touch the baby, don't touch the baby." She didn't have much to do with me after that, deciding early on that I was going to be nothin' but trouble.

Carleen, laying me on the dining room table to change my diapers, turned to get them from the sideboard's bottom drawer while ordering Claudia to keep an eye on me. Claudia, leaning against the wall with her arms crossed, calmly watched as I rolled right off the table and bounced onto the wood floor. She got slapped and hollered at for not watching me. Oh she was watching me all right, she just wasn't about to touch me.

My fair-haired sister was no longer the baby of the family, had lost her mother's attention, was now forbidden to suck her thumb, and wasn't one bit happy about any of it. While Mom held me, I sucked the two middle fingers on my left hand and rubbed her earlobe with my right. When she gave me cotton balls to rub between my fingers instead, Claudia sulked, "Mom never bought me any damn cotton balls."

Claudia

6. Birds of a Feather • 1948, Sonora, California

Lorna Harrington, Betty's best friend since kindergarten, was unusually shy. My sister took her under her wing from the beginning, and now as eight-year-old birds of a feather, they flew everywhere together.

A pair of mini-tornados, they whirled up one side of Washington Street and zipped

Lorna   Betty

down the other, poking their head in every store, peering down every byway, and peeking in all the tavern windows to see what was going on. On Saturdays they flew up the steep steps of St. Patrick's, and in cahoots, slipped into the silent and empty church. While Betty sifted through the religious tracts standing upright in the wood rack, Lorna stood lookout at the sanctuary entrance doors: her parents were atheists. Betty culled the pamphlets; all the ones not in accordance with her views, she tossed in a trash can conveniently located right next to the rack. She felt there was no need for people to be squandering their time reading dogma and doctrine that was just plain wrong.

One late Saturday afternoon, Father Gilmartin caught the pair of little heathens.

"Unless you two are here for Mass, you are no longer welcome in this church."

But they didn't care. Cackling, the duo flew down the stone steps and gusted over to Elsbree's Cigar Store to hide in the magazine bin and read the comic books.

Spending hours under the oak in the vacant lot across from Lorna's house, Betty and Lorna told stories, read books, and studied the dictionary from cover to cover, testing each other until they knew the meaning and origin of every word from aardvark to zoology. The two fast friends collected weird and wonderful words like other kids collected bubble gum cards.

Swinging her legs over the porch rail and jumping to the ground, Betty raced to Lorna's and they'd be off for the day. They trudged miles upstream to catch giant leopard frogs in the creek, then toted them home in gunnysacks tossed over their shoulders, selling them to the

Sonora Inn for fried frogs' legs, making five cents a frog. They had tea parties in tiny secret hideaways carved inside the row of hedges lining the back yard. They skated the streets, hiked the hills, and dared each other to climb rock walls and tall trees. As the sidewalks all over town were fractured from tree roots, the only good place to skate was in front of the courthouse; they were forever being chased off during business hours. Hand-in-hand, they skipped along the cracked sidewalks, Lorna hanging onto her glasses, singing radio jingles off-key at the top of their lungs: *Brusha, brusha, brusha, get the new Ipana...*

A Business Section. No 1. Sonora, Calif.

7. Holy Cards, Hell, and High Water • Summer 1949, Sonora

Sonora was a backwater with no Catholic school, so every summer five young Franciscan nuns in black habits and white wimples were imported to bring the schoolchildren a proper Catholic education. The Sisters did their best to inoculate the youngsters, dispensing a heaping dose of guilt to tide them over to the next summer. Larry, Carleen, and Betty had already built up an immunity; the majority of the teachings simply washed over them like a fine, quickly evaporating mist. Claudia was still impressionable, taking all the teachings to heart.

During catechism, as rewards for knowing the right answers, the nuns gave out felt scapulars and scores of holy cards. Claudia collected the most, knowing nearly all the answers. She took no duplicates. "No, I already have that one, thank you." She wore her scapular every day. After a month, when the felt strap and backing got too ratty, the Sacred Heart of Mary and the face of Christ looking upwards towards God were carefully folded and tucked away in her underwear drawer.

In the beginning, Claudia was a believer, but by the third grade, skepticism was gaining ground. During catechism she had many questions: "How could the blood and body of Christ be in a wafer that came in a box from the post office? Would you really get blood in your mouth if you bit into one? How come only men get to be priests? Did God say that?"

She didn't get any satisfactory answers, other than somehow most of this was Eve's fault: our downfall began with her. The explanations she gleaned from the nuns were, "Some things you simply have to take on faith," or "it is a mystery; no one knows the answer," responses which simply increased her confusion. When she double-checked with Mom, her comeback was generally, "Well, that's just the way it is."

One day a nun stopped Claudia and patted her eight-year-old head as she came out of the Sonora Library. "What a pious child you are!" Sister Bernadette beamed at her. "You'll grow up and be a perfect nun."

Alarmed, Claudia ran home and tore through the screen door. "I have to be a nun!" she cried. "I don't want to be a nun!" Throwing herself against Mother, she relayed what Sister had said.

"Oh, for the love of God, Claudia, you don't have to be a nun," Mom pooh-poohed, much to Claudia's great relief. "You can be whatever you want to be when you grow up. Now go outside. I'm trying to get dinner on."

Mother spent much of her time countermanding what the church professed.

"Don't be ridiculous, you're not going to hell if you eat meat on Friday," she'd snort, cleaning her glasses and shaking her head.

"No, you won't go to hell if you don't go to Mass on Sunday," throwing her arms in the air in disdain. "And no, you won't go to hell if you walk into a Protestant church."

"But those are all mortal sins!" Claudia cried, "Like murder!"

Mom clamped her hands on both hips in scorn. "That's all a crock of hooey!"

"But they said…" my sister wailed in response.

"Oh for heaven's sake, Claudia," and mother, rolling her eyes, launched into another exposition on hell, high water, and common sense.

Claudia and Mom, Sonora

The first time our mother left was in April, 1950, before I was two. Claudia was seven years older than I was, so that made her eight; Betty was ten, Carleen was fifteen, and Larry sixteen.

Carleen snapped at us, "For the umpteenth time, I don't know why she left, when we'll see her again, or where she went, and no, I don't know if she's coming back. Now don't ask any more questions!"

Our lives continued.

Claudia, Carleen, Larry, Betty, Cathy in front
1950, Sonora

Spring faded. Summer passed. Fall blew into winter. Mom returned once for a week, wept the whole time she was home, then fled again. She came back a few times more, but knew she couldn't live a life she didn't want. She told Larry she didn't know what to do, that she'd go crazy if she didn't get away, that she had to leave.

A lot happened in the family during that time: Daddy could no longer hold his head up in town, kids were told not to play with my sisters, and people whispered. A lot of it had to do with sex, the very thing my father couldn't tolerate, especially when it had to do with anyone in the family.

Finally, in 1952, packing what she could carry in two suitcases, Mom left for good. Mothers didn't run away in those days, except ours did, and Betty never forgave her.

Even though she hated Mom, Betty was miserable without her. She didn't want to go to school and complained that her throat hurt. After too many weeks of absences, Daddy decided she needed her tonsils out.

Carleen, age 16, 1950, Sonora

When summer arrived, it was time. Carleen woke us up on Tuesday and told us to get dressed. That day, Claudia was signed up for a novice tennis tournament sponsored by the recreation department; Carleen told her she wasn't going to be able to play, we were going somewhere with Daddy. She didn't tell us where. When we drove to the Columbia Way Hospital, Daddy was waiting at the entrance. He informed us we were having our tonsils taken out. Since Betty needed hers out, he decided both Claudia and I might as well have ours removed, too.

"Who's first?" the nurse asked.

Betty and Claudia pointed to me. My not quite four-year-old body was packed up and carried howling down the short corridor as my sisters listened to my screams. My wailing was muffled, then silent, from the metal cone of ether held over my face. Claudia was next.

When we all came to, we were told not to throw up or cough because we could bleed to death, as if we had a choice about not throwing up. Of course we all threw up, and did so for days afterwards, sick from the ether, certain we were going to die, and wishing we would. It took me the longest to recover. That was the beginning of my several hospital stays, and the end of Claudia's tennis career.

9. A Defining Moment • December 1953, San Jose, California

I don't remember how I got there or who dropped me off, perhaps Daddy waited in a car across the street, or maybe the family I'd been living with brought me. Who knows? It didn't really matter; I was coming to live with my mother! I bunny-hopped on her doorstep, the butterflies in my stomach on the wing. Not tall enough to reach the knocker, I rapped twice on the door. She would be so happy to see me!

The front door opened. Standing there, she glanced over my head. She stepped back and let me pass, then closed the door and turned. Picking up my small yellow and white, brown-striped suitcase, I trailed after her.

Working as a cook and housekeeper for two Irish Catholic priests, my mother lived in a small room off the church's rectory. She led me to the dining room and pointed to a place at the end of the pew against a wall, then disappeared into the kitchen through the white Dutch-door.

Her voice tight, she ordered, "Be quiet and behave," followed by, "sit there and don't touch anything."

With my Naugahyde case deposited on the floor under the pew, I dangled my feet, sitting very still on the hard bench, obediently folding my five-year-old hands in my lap. I studied the red-flocked wallpaper, the tatted doilies, the long rectangular dining table set for two: the wine goblets, silver spoons, the scatter of white plates, linen, crystal, and pewter… all waiting in silence, like me. Wondering how I got there and pretty sure I hadn't done anything wrong, I'd wait most of my life for her to come back to me. She never did.

10. Perms

Carleen always gave us a Toni the day before school pictures; she was making us beautiful. She shampooed us, yanked our snarls, swore at us to quit sniveling, then sat us in a row at the yellow Formica kitchen table. With old bath towels draped over our shoulders, Betty, Claudia and I perched on the matching vinyl chairs, waiting our turn. Carleen scotch-taped our wet bangs to our foreheads, then with Mom's good sewing scissors, snipped them straight across. Starting at the crowns of our heads, she carefully wrapped each combed lock with a little white square of tissue paper, then tightly rolled it in pink plastic rods, ordering us to, "sit still and quit whining." Finally, she poured the processing solution over our heads, tilting her head sideways so she wouldn't pass out from the reek of ammonia. We held the cotton strips tight to our forehead so we wouldn't go blind.

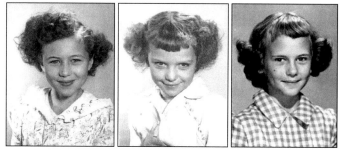

Betty, 1951   Claudia, 1951   Cathy, 1958

By morning, our bangs had shrunk three inches above our eyebrows, four inches where the cowlicks were. Flat on top, the rest of our hair was so tight and curly it stuck out in triangles on each side like Bozo the Clown, but one side was always higher than the other, so it looked like our hair was on crooked. We also stank to high heaven for a week.

One year, the year I was six and Carleen wasn't around, Mom put Betty and Claudia in charge of my hair. Leaving the barbershop in tears, my sisters made me trail ten feet behind, saying I looked like a boy and so ugly they couldn't be seen with me, laughing and taunting, "We don't even know you," and calling me a, "poor little orphan girl."

However, I think my hair did look better in my school picture that year.

Cathy, 1954

11. Zane Grey and Nancy Drew

I never thought of myself as abused (no one ever slapped me), or as a latchkey kid (we never locked our door), but Mom wasn't around much in the five years I lived with her. When she was, she escaped into sleep, her small feather pillow and black eye mask blocking out the world. As a small girl, I watched her from the edge of the room, keeping vigil, waiting for her to rise from the void.

Cathy, 1st grade

Our eyes were the same color, a speckled hazel, but Mother's were vacant. Sometimes she gave a little start and looked surprised when I walked through her line of vision, as if she forgot I lived there too. It wasn't that she didn't like me, she was, well, she was simply indifferent. Perhaps it wasn't even indifference; maybe it was the pills, or her bad eyes. She was myopic, almost blind without her glasses. Whatever it was, the only person my mother was aware of was herself, dancing in her own galaxy to a drummer no one else could hear. It was confusing, wondering what she was thinking, attempting to make her happy, trying to figure out if she was even in there.

We shared a bed. It was soothing sleeping next to her, not so lonely. I remember one time when I was sick, she let me rest my head on her soft stomach. As she turned the pages of her book, I listened to the sounds inside her, the gurgling and churning and popping commotion in her belly, the cadence of her heart and the passage of her breath. I wanted nothing more than to feel the rise and fall of her, to close my eyes and experience her warmth. She didn't seem to mind. I loved the smell of her too; she smelled of Pond's with a dusting of Lily of the Valley.

When she wasn't sleeping, she hid between the covers of books. Mother read everything, from hardcover historical fiction to paperback pulp: Zane Grey and Louis L'Amour were staples. Her favorite magazines spanned *True Crime* and *Detective Story* to *Reader's Digest* and *Coronet*; she flipped through those while

Noreen "Babe" Clemens

she ate. I loved reading, too. I read the backs of cereal boxes and our giant dictionary. Later, I disappeared into *Nancy Drew* and *The Hardy Boys*. We carried stacks of books home from the library, as many as we could tote without spilling words on the sidewalk. Reading saved us; it gave us other people's lives to live.

12. Dick and Jane • 1955, San Jose, California

Jefferson Elementary was like all grammar schools: the classrooms arranged with five rows of seven metal wood-topped desks; the playground as barren and flat as a prison yard; the morning and midday recesses echoing the cacophony of unruly children.

Jefferson Elementary School, 1955, San Jose

I remember a lot about second grade: the finger-paints, watercolors, and pull-down maps, the damp winter cloakroom piled with dripping raincoats and soggy boots, the screech of chalk, ticking clock, and the whirl of the sharpener spewing pencil dust on the wall by Miss Harrison's desk. I can still smell the white paste and buff paper with wood chinks and blue lines. I even recall the taste: the flaky crumbs and gummy texture of graham crackers washed down with a half-pint container of milk, and the taste of chewed Ticonderoga pencils.

I remember Dick and Jane.

"See Jane run. Run Jane, run."

I knew exactly how Jane felt. I wanted to run too.

We had monthly fire drills, holding hands two-by-two, boys in one line, girls in the other, marching away from the low, one-story building built like a bunker. During air-raid practices we crouched like rolled up pill-bugs under our desks, our arms protecting our heads. But there was never a nuclear attack, and even if there was, it was unlikely that an inch-thick desktop was going to protect me. Oh please… I had enough real dangers in my life to fret about.

There were things I liked about second grade, and things I didn't. I didn't like sitting smack dab in the center of the middle row of desks. Praying no one would notice me, I kept my eyes lowered, fingering the skate key I wore around my neck like a rosary, aching to suck my fingers. Terrified of being caught and called a baby, I chewed my nails or orange pencils instead.

One of the things I didn't like was the playground. The swings and merry-go-round made me queasy and the jungle gym and high bar scared me to death. The teeter-totter was dangerous, especially when the fat, redheaded kid with glasses thought it a riot to roll off sideways when he was at the bottom and I was at the top.

I liked reading stories and practicing letters, and staying inside when it rained. I liked drawing and the feel of smooth paper and the smell of waxy crayons. I always drew the same house: it had a peaked roof, a green door, one window, a big tree to the left, a lemon yellow sun shining in the upper right, and a row of red tulips in front.

What I liked the most was lunch. Eating my peanut butter and jelly sandwich, my three Oreo cookies, and a small red box of Sunmaid raisins, I balanced myself on the cement curb at the far corner of the playground. Hunching my shoulders and raking my heels back and forth, making small hollows in the bald hardpack, I sat by myself and watched the other girls play four-square and hopscotch. Some days, Kendra, whose parents were deaf mutes, sat with me. I fed my crusts to the blackbirds and gave Kendra my raisins; they made my cavities hurt.

Kendra taught me to sign. One day, from her blouse pocket, she presented me with a small folded card that showed me how to hold my hands for each letter so I could practice on my own. I thought maybe I could teach Mom, maybe break the silence another way. But my mother wasn't interested; the only voices heard in our house were the ones in her head.

13. High Crime • 1956, San Jose, California

"I am Mother or Mom! Not Ma!"

That was the only time I remember my mother being cross with me. She never got after me for not brushing my teeth or knocking over my milk, and she didn't punish me for being a thief. She didn't care about such things; actually, she didn't notice such things. But she did get after me for calling her "Ma."

She had to know I was stealing, because at eight years old and not gainfully employed, I had no money and a pile of new toys. I'd stolen a complete line of Storybook dolls, their clothes, shoes, and accessories; I'd also swiped a stash of Crayolas and marbles, along with jacks, slingshots, and squirt guns. I went with Kendra. We sat playing on the floor of the toy aisle deciding what to pilfer, then would casually stuff our cache of the day down our panties or inside our sweaters and calmly saunter out the front door of the five-and-dime. We were the store's most loyal shoplifters.

Willow Glen Elementary School, 1956, San Jose
(Cathy, center in second row from top)

After a couple of weeks of high crime, I got caught. Facing the checkout register to pay for a pack of gum while tucking a bag of colored balloons in the back of my pants, a large hand grabbed my shoulder. I broke out in a sweat. The storeowner jerked the balloons out of my pocket, spun me around, grabbed my arm, and shoved me out the door.

"If I ever see your face in here again, I'll call the cops!"

I quit stealing after that, not so much because it was a grave sin, but because I knew in my heart it wasn't right. And the truth is, I never wanted to get caught again. At eight, being sent to jail was more than I could imagine. Besides, I could go back to confession with a clean conscience.

14. An 8" x 10" Glossy • June 1956, Upland, California

The first time my parents saw each other after their divorce was at Larry and Marian's wedding. I have an 8" x 10" glossy reminder of the occasion: the respective parents are flanking the bride and groom, Marian's parents to her right, smiling big and happy, Larry's to his left, looking, well, just looking. Mom, white-hatted and gloved, bejeweled and corsaged, appears pleased through her cat-eye glasses. Daddy, who was Larry's best man, is tight-lipped and granite-jawed. My father's tie is sticking out, looking as ruffled and trapped as he is.

Marian's parents, Marian, Larry, Mom and Dad

The plot had thickened. Mom was married to Ray and Daddy had married Irene, a woman nineteen years his senior with an uncanny resemblance to his mother impersonating Mae West. Irene was a well-dressed matron whose downtown attire was a suit, high heels, hat and gloves, and whose cocktail apparel consisted of gowns, silk hose, furs, and diamonds. If you lived in San Francisco in the fifties, you dressed for it. She moved in a cloud of face powder. Her false eyelashes and kohl-lined eyes slightly sagged above the layers of red lipstick that leaked into the lines around her lips. She had bleached blonde curly hair and smelled like a mix of heavy perfume and mothballs. Irene was the toast of the San Francisco cocktail circuit—married to my conservative, not-much-of-a-drinker father. If he had more than two highballs, he got sicker than a poisoned pup.

It was better that Irene wasn't there for Larry's wedding. When she saw the pictures of her husband standing next to his former wife, she was foot-stomping furious. She didn't want any reminders that he'd been married before, or that he had children. It was a good thing Daddy and his tie looked so nervous.

Carl and Irene Clemens
1956, New Year's Eve
San Francisco

When they married, Dad moved to Irene's upper flat, a two-story Victorian just a couple doors up from where he'd been renting on Belvedere. It was furnished with carved antiques and Persian rugs, hung with oil paintings and gilded mirrors, and filled with crystal and china. She had a cold storage room built between the living room and dining room for her two walls of full-length minks, silver fox stoles, and black sable jackets. The end portion had built-in shelves from floor to ceiling, stacked with beautiful round hatboxes.

I stayed three days with Daddy during that first summer he and Irene were married; I was seven, nearly eight. My recollection of her was me getting caught rummaging through the old trunks in her basement, wanting to play dress-up, but only looking at her carefully packed-away clothes. Well, maybe I did hold a couple of them up in front of me to see how they looked. Okay, so I tried one on. She was livid.

Irene was gracious to Larry and Marian, but didn't bother to hide her jealousy of her husband's daughters. When Carleen and Chuck drove up for a weekend visit and had dinner at Alioto's in Fisherman's Wharf, Irene kept her back to Carleen at the bar. She ignored my sister the entire evening and didn't even look at her. Not once.

We didn't see much of Daddy in the three years he was married to Irene. The few times he visited us in La Habra he came by himself. He explained it would simply be easier.

15. Smoke Gets in Your Eyes • 1959, La Habra, California

Sequestered by the murky outline of the San Gabriel Mountains, Orange County had constant smog alerts, sometimes so bad they closed the schools. Everyone was told to stay indoors, the outside smothered in a pea soup of brown haze so dense not even a Santa Ana wind could blow it away.

The pall enveloping our card games was worse than the pall outside. Carleen inhaled Pall Malls and Claudia smoked Salems. Betty preferred Parliaments, and when she was full of herself, she smoked Vogues. She smoked two, three, sometimes four packs a day, blowing me perfect smoke rings whenever I asked.

In those days, everyone smoked: Ricky and Lucy, John Wayne, Grace Kelly, Ed Sullivan, Liberace, my sixth grade teacher Mrs. Wilcox, my mother, and my three sisters.

Carleen, Claudia, Betty, Larry, Cathy, circa 1959, La Habra

I was happiest when playing cards with my sisters. The four of us sat at the dining table for hours, their oldest kids locked outside the front screen door to play in the neighborhood, the babies in the playpens napping while we shuffled, cut, and dealt. They let me play because they needed a fourth for partner Hearts, Canasta, or Pinochle.

I didn't interfere with their conversation and I laughed at their jokes, which were over my head. I ingratiated myself by serving them ham sandwiches, refilling coffee, lighting their cigarettes, and emptying ashtrays. Some weekends we'd be at it all day and all night, only taking breaks to feed the kids. Betty lost a babysitter once because she didn't make it home until dawn. "One more hand," we'd say, "just one more hand."

They drank pot after pot of coffee and smoked pack after pack of filters, complaining the whole time how crappy their hands were, bad-mouthing Mother, and bitching about their husbands. I was clear that I did not like coffee or cigarettes, clear that I was not going to grow up to be like Mom, and really clear I wasn't going to marry some s.o.b. like they had.

Playing a game of Hearts, I carefully organized my cards by suit and value, alternating the reds and blacks, trying not to drop any face up on the table, when it dawned on me what I had. I held the Queen of Spades, all the high hearts, and enough lower ones to shoot the moon. Yabba dabba doo!

"Yessss!" I hid my crooked grin behind my fanned cards, so excited I could barely contain myself, my brown cowlicks and peepers popping with glee.

"Whooeee!" I slapped my free hand on the table.

"Yaahooo!" my butt cheeks danced on the chair.

"Oh yeahhh!"

Swearing, the three of them threw in their cards and didn't let me play my hand.

Cathy, 5th grade, La Habra

"I hate you!" I whined.

"Oh shut up and shuffle," they replied.

There's nothing like a common enemy to unite sisters, and we had Mom. Our mother's redeeming value though was, she played cards. When she pulled up in her black-and-white Buick Special with the four chrome holes on its sides, we readied ourselves. Carleen and Betty said they didn't like being stuck with her as a partner either, but since *either* had to go to school during the day, they tolerated her as my fill-in. They cheated when they played with Mom, slightly fanning their cards to each other, quietly passing under the table whatever they needed to fill out their hand. Mom wasn't as sharp as she once was. Her thinking ability was fuzzy from shock treatments and the pills that she took, and my sisters took full advantage.

Mom, La Habra

Whenever they talked about Mom, they referred to her as *your* mother, like she wasn't *their* mother, just mine.

I learned a lot more from playing cards than just shuffling, cutting, and dealing, like how to win and how to lose. I realized that pouting didn't improve my hand one whit. I got the hang of the rules, how to keep score, and how to count. I learned how to bluff. I mastered keeping my cards close to my chest, when to hold 'em, and when to fold 'em. I learned to lead with my strong suits, and to play my bad cards as well as I could. I got cheating wasn't fair, or all that much fun. I learned to play the cards dealt me even when they were rotten, and that it was only a game and not to take it too seriously. I learned about the Ace of Hearts and the Queen of Spades, and that hearts trump everything and hope trumps anything. And I learned that there was always a new hand soon to be dealt, and possibly, a better one.

16. Sprouse Reitz • San Francisco, 1960 to 1968

During the summers I worked in my dad's dime store, saving my earnings for milkshakes, school clothes, and college. He taught me how to work as soon as I was old enough to be employed.

First, he showed me how to maneuver the giant push broom up and down the aisles. Next, how to stock shelves, track inventory, run the register, and then, how to wait on customers and watch for shoplifters. He broke it down one job at a time, and didn't give me a new task until I learned to do the last one. I liked working. I got to be with my dad.

I worked half days at first. Daddy let me sit, maybe because I was young, or maybe because I looked pale. If I stood for too long, my stomach hurt. I had a constant gnawing inside me. When my anxiety got worse, it escalated to a swarm of grasshoppers. When it got too bad, when it felt like I had a horde of locusts ricocheting off my insides and I doubled over, Daddy took me to a doctor who said I had pancreatitis, put me on a low-fat diet, and also suggested I stay out of the store's candy bins. Changing what I ate helped.

I seldom ventured beyond the store, so whatever ambled in was my sum total experience of the larger world. I remember one late June afternoon, a boy, not quite my age, maybe fourteen—slender, blonde, and nervous—needed help. He wanted to buy a bra. Too embarrassed, especially when I realized he wanted it for himself, I summoned Daddy. At that age, I wouldn't even look at a boy, much less help one buy a brassiere. I disappeared to the back of the store to check on the paint cans. My father fitted him, rang him up, bagged his purchase (two 32AAA), politely thanked him, and never batted an eyelash.

The next day, a couple of tall, brassy, black bombshells with high cleavage and spiked heels promenaded through the front doors and over to the yardage section, browsing the Butterick patterns and dime store velvet. The regular customers preferred solid cotton and calico, unless it was Christmas or New Years.

As the redhead fingered the shiny sateen and taffeta, the bleached blonde settled on scarlet velveteen. While I ran the bolt through the metal measuring machine anchored to the pullout shelf, I surreptitiously observed them from the corner of my eye as they picked out two spools of matching crimson thread. Their Adam's apples and large hands didn't catch my attention until I rang up their purchases. Across the counter, I checked out their wigs, false eyelashes, arched eyebrows, red lipstick, and faces heavy on the pancake makeup. As they sashayed out the front doors, primly adjusting their tight miniskirts, they both turned and threw me a wink and a kiss.

Daddy elbowed me, nearly knocking me over. "Quit gawking," he said, out of the corner of his mouth, barely moving his lips. I couldn't help it. I'd never seen a transvestite. And for the second time in two days, I was stunned my father didn't raise an eyebrow. For a man who made it abundantly clear that anything sexual was indecent, improper, and immoral, it simply didn't compute.

17. The Summer of Love • 1967, San Francisco

1967 was the Summer of Love, and nearly 100,000 people from across America and beyond descended on the Haight-Ashbury, joining the flower power phenomenon that had erupted in San Francisco, creating a media circus and a social earthquake. In search of the holy grail of sex, drugs, and rock and roll, they joined the spiral dance, swapping flowers, love, and sex, for peyote, mushrooms, and mescaline. The boys in Nehru jackets, tie-dyed shirts, and paisley bell-bottoms and the girls in flowing skirts, patched jeans, and braless tops were experiencing a whole new world through granny glasses and windowpanes of blotter acid. On a cosmic peace train, they wanted to stop the war, stoned on love, love, love. Renouncing consumerism and materialism, they came in the store to steal ribbon, gum, and balloons. The throng of barefoot long-haired kids, tripping on purple haze and orange sunshine, represented everything my father stood against. Daddy hated the Summer of Love.

Every morning, runaway teenagers from Des Moines, Dayton, and Duluth slept in the storefront. My father had to step around them in the early morning fog to open up, muttering, "Goddam good-for-nothin' dirty hippies." After mopping the store aisles, he'd haul the bucket out front and dump the raunchy mop water on them. Later in the day he'd take his big push broom and sweep them off the sidewalk as they napped in the afternoon sun.

A policeman tried to stop him once. "You can't do that, Mr. Clemens," he said, holding his hand up to halt my father.

"When I see shit," Daddy retorted, "I sweep it in the gutter where it belongs." With a final push, he turned on his heel and walked back inside. My father seldom swore, except when provoked by shoplifters and hippies.

In the aftermath of the Be-In and the Summer of Love, the Haight slid straight downhill. The originators of the counterculture movement had fled, and the deteriorating Victorians were now a mixture of psychedelic-colored crash pads and rundown heroin haunts. An element of criminals and pimps populated the streets, the rows of empty store windows plastered with Free Love, Free Food, and Free Huey handbills. Dime stores didn't do well in that grittier climate. None of the old neighborhood stores did.

The Grayline tour busses tootled past what used to be the Haight Theatre and was now the Straight Theatre, overflowing with flabby, white–thighed Midwesterners in tank tops and Bermuda shorts. The tourists leaned out the windows like bird-watchers, binoculars and cameras hanging from their necks, some hoping to catch a glimpse of the few remaining hippies, others praying to spot their runaway children.

My dad managed the Sprouse-Reitz store at 1644 Haight Street from 1954 until its doors closed in 1968. Adding great insult to my father's injury, the Haight-Ashbury Free Clinic moved in, and the hippies and addicts—hoping for some spare change and a ray of sun in the morning fog, could finally rest in peace against the red and gray tiled storefront.

Daddy, Arboretum in San Francisco

18. Positively Haight Street • 1968

 1968 was the year Eldridge Cleaver published Soul on Ice. He and his wife Kathleen, who had the most immense head of hair I'd ever laid eyes on, banked at my teller window. It was the year of the Yippies, Black Panthers, and the SDS, the year Martin Luther King was shot in Memphis—sparking riots across the nation. The day after his murder, hundreds of black kids from Poly High rolled down Haight in a tidal wave, smashing storefront windows and overturning cars.

1968 was the year of the sweeping anti-war protests, the Tet Offensive and the My Lai Massacre, the year the Viet Nam war ripped our country inside out. It was the year of the Democratic National Convention and the Chicago riots. Sirhan Sirhan assassinated Bobby Kennedy at the Los Angeles Ambassador Hotel, women were branded as bra-burning feminists, and 32 African nations boycotted the Summer Olympics in Mexico City. Richard Nixon was elected president, and Apollo 7 and 8 were launched.

 I existed in the eye of this turbidity— not oblivious—but not overly concerned or connected to the world's chaos. Dressed in my starched white button-down collared blouse, navy A-line skirt, pantyhose, white flats, Coral Sea lipstick and a helmet-head Summer-Blonde flip, I watched with detached interest the swirl of humanity through the plate glass windows of my dad's five-and-dime and the corner bank across the street.

In my world, 1968 was the year the neighborhood stores closed, leaving empty shells with boarded windows. Customers were fed up with grungy panhandlers constantly asking for spare change to feed their mangy bandana-necked dogs, tired of stepping over stoned fourteen-year-old runaways who looked like five miles of blank road, and had it with being hustled by dreadlocked junkies, spaced-out punks, and blissed-out barefoot bums. The regulars hailed streetcars to Irving or took the bus over to Market, then eventually moved out of the Haight altogether.

1968 was the year Daddy's store closed. The Summer of Love, the riots, and the changing times did my father's business in. I find it worthwhile to note that his history echoed the same song from fifteen years earlier, the times again cracking my Dad's foundation and walls. Once again he sold his stock, boarded his windows, locked his glass front doors, and—once again—left town.

1968 was also the final straw for my mother. That was the year she ended her life in a small hotel on Whittier Boulevard, closing a chapter on mine.

19. A Billet-Doux to My Siblings, written in 2004

Dear Gordon (Larry) and Marian, Carleen, Liz (Betty), and Claudia,

My writing began with "Queen Bee." When I shared it with each of you, it gave us a connection we hadn't had. I also read it to our cousin Marceline whom I'd met at a Chatfield reunion a few years back, where she told me stories about Mom: how warm, friendly and funny Mother was. It startled me to hear anyone say anything good about Mom, to hear her spoken of in such a friendly fashion. Carleen and Liz, your anger with Mother had been so intractable, and my own experience of her difficult, that I thought perhaps Marceline was mixing her up with someone else.

Clemens siblings: Carleen, Gordon "Larry", Catherine "Cathy", Liz "Betty", Claudia, 1993

I'd reconnected with Marceline a year ago, and I invited her and the five of you to my home. I wanted to know more about our mother. Thirty others got wind of the get-together and showed up on my doorstep, arms loaded with food and soft drinks; it turned into a wonderful weeklong party. Four generations—brothers, sisters, cousins, nieces, nephews, children and grandchildren—sat in a double circle in my living room. I asked everyone in turn to say how they were related to Mom, along with a memory or story of her. That night I wrote out the tales told and read them aloud in the morning. Everyone thought my writings were funny, except you, Gordon—you weren't so sure—but then, you had a different family life than we did. Those few tales triggered others, and then others, and when they'd all been written down, I had a book. Chronicled throughout are diaries, letters, and clippings stashed for years in your closets. My own memories and assumptions are cluttered in between.

Relieved when I got your first responses to my draft, Carleen, Liz, Claudia, and Marian, you all said, "I laughed, then I cried, then I laughed some more." I worried what you would say, Gordon. Until you'd read my first draft, you'd only heard what I'd read to you on the phone. I often felt your pursed lips and folded arms over the line. The day I received your edited copy, I was afraid to unseal the manila envelope. I circled it for an hour, tapping it with my fingers each time I walked by the kitchen table, waiting for courage to open it. I didn't want to risk our relationship, you're the only brother I have.

I cried when your note said my writing impressed you, and that you hadn't known what had happened to all of us after you'd left home. You also didn't ask me to take anything out, except where I wrote that you had hunted for frogs, informing me that you had NEVER hunted for frogs. I also laughed when I saw you had crossed out all the swear words. And I want to thank you for your generosity in allowing me to print something so personal as your diary; it tied the story together.

Marian and Gordon

Marian, you have been a huge support, reading drafts and running interference. You loved my writing and asked me if I was ever going to write fiction. My brother—your husband—responded with, "She is writing fiction." What I love the most about you is your kindness and patience. You soften my edges, reminding me by your example of another way to be.

Carleen, thank you for being our mother when Mom was not able, to not only take us in and provide food and shelter, but to give us love, laughter, attention, and family. Your home and heart were always open, and I might not be here today if not for you.

Liz, thanks for putting up with me on the phone, sometimes two and three times a day, patiently listening, correcting, and making me take out what I made up. "Riddled with errors, as usual," you'd quip. Your memory, knowledge, and stand for the truth make a difference. I'm also grateful you're still speaking to me after I decided, against your request, to include some painful things that happened to you when you were young. I can only trust it was the right decision.

Claudia, your stories have been the best. You had the closest connection with Mom (actually, you were the only one with the fortitude to listen to her), so you have memories the rest of us lack. I laugh each time we talk, and feel your arm around me. I hope I'm not still "nothin' but trouble" for you with what I've written.

What I thought would be a few vignettes has turned into this memoir, reaching back through our generations and growing into a  body of work. I wrote it for you, and I wrote it for me. It gave me a place to say what I wanted to say, it brought me clarity and tenderness as I witnessed my childhood, and it brought me back to myself. It also united our family in more ways than just these pages. I've always said, "If it had been up to me, I'd have kept the family together." Well, I've done that, and then some.

With love, Catherine

20. Queen Bee • March, 2002

I am the Queen Bee. You know how I know? My friends tell me. I've been called the Carrot Juice Queen, the Dance Floor Queen, and the Queen of Sonoma Real Estate. I am also known as Her Highness in my family, Her Oneness in class, and Her Eminence at my work.

I am the Queen of Complaint and the Queen of Control. And why not? This world would be a much better place if everyone would just do it my way. Besides, if I didn't try to control everything, well, who would? It might just all fall apart! I am clear it's up to me to be in charge. It's the Queen's job!

Queen Bee

I am also the Queen of Funny. Every once in a while though, I hang out with my sons, just to make sure I don't get too queenly. You see, my sons don't think I'm so funny. Maybe I just have a timing problem with them. One time I sent my younger son a cartoon; in it, this therapist is slapping his patient upside the head telling him to "Snap out of it!" The caption in the corner reading, SINGLE SESSION THERAPY. My son's response? "You think that's funny?" I thought it was hilarious. Apparently he didn't.

I'm also the Queen of Confusion. I know right from left because I salute the flag with my right hand. But a sense of direction never translated to my feet. In dance class my teacher would say, "now come forward on your right foot" and I'd do that, and my partner would lean into me and whisper politely, "your other right foot." I do know up from down, however. Look, there are plenty of gas stations out there if I ever need more directions than that.

Last week, my bones were aching so much I went to see a healer. "Your bones are fine," he said, "it's your mother. She hasn't passed over yet, and she needs your help to get to the other side." He told me that she was my spirit guide and said that I had a lot of work to do soon and would need her help, and that she couldn't help me until her journey was complete. He said to put food and water for her on my altar every day, to pray for her and for my ancestors before I went to sleep at night.

As a kid, I knew I wasn't a queen and it didn't seem to matter if I was there or not; sometimes I'd sneak a look in the mirror to see if I really existed. I thought something must have been wrong with me, and if I could be perfect, well, I might be able to fix what was wrong.

I've wired it up for almost fifty years to protect this Queen of Hearts and it's taking some time to undo these bindings, piece by piece. I have to be careful as I think my heart might be cracked as it hurts so much sometimes. But I have help: I have honeybees in my heart, making honey from my fear, shame, resentment, and guilt. I now know I have the heart of a queen, filled with courage and love. You know how I know? My friends tell me. And when I take a peek in the mirror—I can see it too.

Catherine (Clemens) Sevenau, 2013, Sonoma

Clemens Family Tree

Carl John Clemens (1905 – 1986)
8th of 13 children of Mathew Sylvester "Matt" Clemens & Barbara Nigon

Married (**1**): Feb 4, 1933, **Noreen Ellen "Babe" Chatfield**, Colusa,
    Colusa Co., California
Divorced: Dec 1953, Sonora, Tuolumne Co., California
Five children: Larry, Carleen, Betty, Claudia, Cathy

Married (**2**): 1956, **Irene V. (Tregear) Whitehead**

Married (**3**): Sep 25, 1961, **Marie Lenore (Macdonald) McCartney**,
    San Francisco, California

Noreen Ellen "Babe" Chatfield (1915 – 1968)
10th of 10 children of Charles Henry Chatfield & Nellie Belle Chamberlin

Married (**1**): Feb 4, 1933, **Carl John Clemens**, Colusa, Colusa Co., California
Divorced: 1953, Sonora, Tuolumne Co., California
Five children: Larry, Carleen, Betty, Claudia, Cathy

Married (**2**): Jul 31, 1955, **Raymond D. "Ray" Haynie**, Carson City,
    Ormsby Co., Nevada
Divorced: 1956, San Jose, Santa Clara Co., California

Five children of Carl John Clemens & Noreen Ellen "Babe" Chatfield:
    1. Gordon Lawrence "Larry" Clemens
        1934 - living
    2. Carleen Barbara Clemens
        1935 - living
    3. Elizabeth Ann "Betty, Liz" Clemens
        1939 - 2004
    4. Claudia Clemens
        1942 - 2011
    5. Catherine Frances "Cathy" Clemens
        1948 – living

37297461R00032

Made in the USA
San Bernardino, CA
15 August 2016